NOAH'S ARK

text by
Christine L. Benagh

Based on a script by Harvey Bullock

ABINGDON PRESS
Nashville

Two young friends, Derek and Margo, are taking part in a very important dig in the Middle East. It is the opportunity of a lifetime for them to accompany her father, an archaeologist, on this expedition.

Most days their young nomad friend Moki, who is very curious about these things, joins them to ask a hundred questions and to keep things generally lively.

One especially hot and tiring day the three friends are digging in their assigned spot, when the sand suddenly begins to give way. "Quicksand," shouts Moki as the three

NOAH'S ARK

Copyright © 1986 by Hanna-Barbera Productions, Inc.

ISBN 0-687-15744-7

MANUFACTURED BY THE PARTHENON PRESS AT NASHVILLE, TENNESSEE, UNITED STATES OF AMERICA

piral down, down, down in a funnel of
and.

Then just as unexpectedly the air is clear,
nd they are in an enormous room. What a
pectacle! It is filled with treasure of every
ort—vases, jars, statues, jewelry and
rnaments, pillars, furniture of gold and
ory.

"How magnificent," whispers Derek in
we.

"Wow," murmurs Moki.

Margo has moved ahead of the others
ward a huge bronze door. The latch
stening the two massive panels is a
olden scarab beetle. She puts her hand on
e scarab, translating its message: *All who
nter here go back in time.* Suddenly, the
reat doors swing open into what appears
be a cavern of light.

"Come on," she calls, and without
esitation the others follow.

They step over the threshold and —

Margo and Derek and Moki found themselves on a narrow road winding through open, peaceful countryside.

However, if they could have seen into the towns around, there was no peace. The towns were filled with danger and fear, violence and murder, thievery and lawlessness.

Men and women, and even children, had no feeling or sympathy for one another. No one was safe in the streets, and it was just as dangerous in one's own home. The cities and families were in ruins and without hope.

The Lord God looked on this cruelty and hate, and he determined to destroy all the creatures he had made.

Only Noah and his family had served God and lived uprightly. God spoke with Noah and told him of his plan to destroy the earth and everything in it by sending a great flood. He instructed Noah to build a large boat, an ark, out of cypress wood, so that he and his family could escape the waters.

The three friends trudged along for what seemed miles. Finally, exhausted, they stopped to rest under a tree beside the road. Almost as soon as they settled down, they were asleep.

Derek awoke to the sound of hammering. "What is that?"

Margo opened her eyes. "Someone must be building something. Let's take a look."

Derek gave Moki a nudge with his foot. "Coming with us?"

Moki only yawned, "I had a great dream going—a giant breakfast with eggs and pancakes and . . ."

"Maybe they're building a house." Derek nudged a little harder.

Moki only rolled over. "So what?"

"A house means a kitchen," Margo began—

Moki was on his feet. "And a kitchen means food!" He was running ahead of the others.

He reached the top of the knoll first and leaned against a large boulder to get his breath. Margo and Derek came up, and they all peered around to discover the source of the sound. They couldn't believe what they saw.

"Wow!" Moki spoke first.

Derek gazed in wonderment. "What kind of house is that?"

Margo also stared and gasped, then suddenly understood. "That's not a house. It's a boat. Do you realize what we are seeing? Noah building his ark!"

"We have to go down there." Derek led the way.

The trio had hardly started down when a figure crept from behind a tree and ducked down beside the boulder. This man, Sebtah, had been waiting for a chance to trouble Noah. He stooped and began to loosen a round stone. His eyes were wild with hate and his clothes in dirty disorder as he tugged and shoved.

At the foot of the hill a woman was taking food from a large basket and putting it on a table set up near the work site. Just above her on the slope was a stack of heavy planks.

Sebtah had pried the stone loose and sent it rumbling down the hill straight into the lumber. The stack swayed and began to lean. The woman screamed when she saw it about to come down on top of her.

Derek and Margo realized what was happening and just had time to rush in and throw their weight against the tottering boards. Moki came puffing up and joined the effort. "Have no fear, Moki is here!" They thrust the lumber back with all their might.

A tall white-haired man came running and put his arm around the woman. "Are you all right, my dear?"

"Yes, Noah," she smiled, "but that was very close. These young people saved my life."

"A boulder rolled down the hill and hit that pile," Moki explained.

Noah nodded. "No doubt that stone had some help from up there." As they looked, a figure darted back to the cover of the tree.

"I am Noah and this is my wife. We are very grateful to you. Tell us, who are you?"

"This is Moki and Derek, and I'm Margo. We are glad to meet you. But tell us, why would anyone want to do such a thing?"

Noah's wife shook her head sadly. "They think we are fools—"

Her husband finished the sentence, "—for building this ark." He pointed to the great hull surrounded by scaffolding.

"That is one huge boat!" Moki turned to the woman. "How many people are working on it, Mrs. Noah—may I call you that?"

"Of course you may," she beamed. "There are eight of us: Noah and me and our sons, Ham, Shem, and Japheth, and their wives."

"How can you do such a big job with so few hands?" Derek wondered aloud. "Couldn't we help?" Moki scowled at him.

"Eight pairs of hands are enough because it is the Lord's will." Noah's voice was resolute. "But you are welcome, my friends, and we will be glad for your help. We have little time before the great flood comes."

"Flood!" gulped Moki. "What are we waiting for? Let's get busy."

They did just that, joining with Noah's family to get the great craft ready. Each day was filled with sawing and hammering, heaving and fitting. Crossbeams were cut, ribs shaped, joints sealed with tar, everything fitted and trimmed according to Noah's instructions.

One afternoon Japheth looked up from his work and groaned, "Here they come again."

"Who?" Derek raised his head to see a band of men approaching.

"These are our 'good' neighbors coming to make jokes about our work." Ham stiffened as he spoke. "Look, Mikab and

Havil and Dedan are with them. This may mean real trouble."

Havil staggered as he stepped out in front of the group, swinging his arms wildly. "Well, well, and what do you suppose this could be?"

"It's big enough to be a barn," Dedan replied laughing.

"You're right," put in Mikab, "and Noah is the biggest donkey of all." A roar of laughter followed this remark.

Noah himself came out to confront the mockers. "Be gone, all of you. You tend to your business and leave us to ours."

Havil shuffled toward Noah. "Attention, everyone." He swayed as he made an unsteady bow. "Hail to the King of Sawdust."

There was more laughter.

Japheth came to Noah's side, clutching a large mallet.

Dedan also made a mocking bow. "Please, O King, tell us what you are going to float this boat on—the dew?"

Noah spoke calmly, "Be warned, all of

you, God has said that floods will soon destroy the earth."

"You don't need to worry, Noah," Mikab called out. "If a flood comes, your hollow head will keep you afloat."

Japheth raised his mallet. "I will not let them talk to you like that, Father."

Noah put a hand on his arm. "Peace, Japheth. They are leaving anyway."

Japheth turned back to the ark. "You know very well they will return with more taunts."

"Perhaps, but do not give them your anger, my son. They need your prayers. The floods are coming and none of them will escape."

Even with these interruptions, the work continued, and the ark grew visibly.

"This is the size of an ocean liner," Derek commented as he handed a board to Shem.

Moki looked up. "One thing is missing—an ocean."

"Noah says the rains are coming," Margo assured him.

He nodded. "It sure is going to take a lot of water to reach up here in the mountains and float a boat like this."

Shem called down, "There will be water, make no mistake, lots of it."

"More rain and water than the earth has ever known," added Ham.

"Suppose it doesn't happen?" Moki had mumbled under his breath, but Derek heard. "Then you'll hear from that bunch of comedians."

Shem came down his ladder and went to the lumber pile. Sebtah was there running his hand along one of the boards. "What are you doing here?"

Ham had also come to the pile. "Are you here to annoy us?"

A hurt look came into Sebtah's eyes. "I am your friend, you know that. I think it is wonderful the way you are helping your father." He took one end of the plank and helped Ham arrange it for sawing.

"You are up to something, and I know it," Ham snapped.

"You wound my feelings," Sebtah pouted. "I am thinking only of your welfare. I want to help you."

"What do you mean?" Shem asked.

"You have all been so busy helping your father that you have neglected your own affairs. You no longer have any land or any cattle, no chance to raise *your* families. It doesn't seem fair somehow." Sebtah started sawing to let this evil hint sink in. Ham and Shem looked at each other with troubled faces.

"But—but—" Ham stammered as he tried to think of something to say, "the ark is important."

"Of course," Sebtah's oily words poured out. "Will the rains come? When? How can you be sure? They may never come, and then what? You will have nothing. What will you do?"

Shem stamped a foot. "We obey Noah!"

"So you should," Sebtah sighed through a thin smile. "Still, if you change your mind, let me know. This is good lumber. I am willing to trade land and cattle for it. Don't you want what is coming to you? Think about it."

"The answer is no!" Noah's sons spoke together.

The false smile disappeared and anger boiled up in Sebtah. "Idiots, all of you, pig-headed idiots. I hope you break your necks on this worthless boat."

It was an especially fine day when Japheth stepped up to Noah and handed him a mallet. "Father, the last board is in place, and you should be the one to set the final peg."

Noah took the mallet and sank to his knees with bowed head. Then he rose, and with a mighty swing, sank the peg. "This great ark, commanded by God and built by men and women, I now pronounce complete." The little company gave a lusty cheer.

Noah raised his hand and continued, "We still have a very important task. We must gather and bring aboard a pair of every living creature on earth."

Without any real gathering, the animals came, as if they had some special feeling about where they should go.

Two giraffes, two elephants, two zebras—Moki had been stationed to take inventory of the animals as they came. Margo and Derek were just inside the great open door where the animals entered, and Noah stood on the deck looking out at the procession of animals, apparently without end, coming to enter the ark.

"Two deer," Margo caressed the doe as she passed, and the creature stopped to nuzzle her hand.

"Two dogs," Moki checked his list. Even before they reached the door the dogs stopped to scratch. "Two fleas," added Moki solemnly.

The animals came two by two, two by two. Then one day as the light was fading, Noah came below deck. "Take care that the animals are bedded down in their stalls; the rains come tomorrow."

"Tomorrow?" Moki's eyes were wide.

"That's what he said." Derek patted Moki's head.

Margo made her way to the deer's stall and fed a handful of straw to her new friend, the doe.

Everyone was on deck first thing the next morning. "Today is the day," said Noah. "Are all things ready?"

"Father!" Japheth came running up. "We cannot close the great outer door. It is too heavy."

"All is in God's hands," Noah said.

"And, Father," Japheth continued, "there is not a cloud in the sky. Are you sure today is the day?"

"All is in God's hands," Noah repeated and turned to leave the deck.

It was a very bright, clear day, and under the warm sun a crowd of unruly people had come out again to tease Noah and his family.

Havil came running up. "We're glad you waited, Noah. We were so afraid you would float away without us."

"Don't worry about us, Noah." It was

Sebtah pretending to swim through water. "We can all swim. Jump in, the water is great."

Mikab shouted, "How many other monkeys do you have in your zoo?"

Noah turned to his company. "Pay them no heed. The rains are coming; they are coming today."

Shem looked up at the cloudless sky and turned to Ham. "The rains will come. He heard God's promise."

Ham looked worried. "What if he did not hear quite right?"

Meanwhile the crowd outside the ark was growing and getting noisier.

"Where are the rain clouds?" Mikab shouted.

Sebtah stepped up. "Yes, Noah, I think you got it wrong. This God of yours is really going to kill us with sunburn."

Havil staggered forward and then turned to the crowd. "C'mon," he croaked. "This big box full of animals would make a great barbecue. Let's set it on fire."

The anxious watchers on the ark heard this, but they could do nothing. "Do not be afraid," Noah said. "Have faith."

Suddenly a loud rumbling was heard. The great door of the ark began to close.

"It is the hand of God." Japheth bowed his head.

Below the crowd was rushing toward the ark. "Let's drag them out of there," Dedan was calling as they ran forward. They too heard the rumble and stopped.

"We can't get at them," said Havil, "the door is closing."

"We can still set the whole thing on fire," snarled Sebtah.

Noah and his company were no longer looking at the angry mob. They were looking at the sky. Heavy banks of black clouds were churning overhead, getting thicker and thicker. A sudden strong wind stunned the crowd and sent them reeling back. The first drops of rain fell, huge and cold.

"It's raining like Noah said!" Havil began to run.

Sebtah grabbed his arm. "Don't be a fool, man. It's only a shower."

On the ark there was one great sigh of relief. Shem stepped up to his father. "I want to admit something. I was beginning to have doubts."

Noah turned to face him. "I know, my son, I too have had them, but all is well, we are in God's hands."

Shem's wife came to Noah's side. "How long will the storm last, Father?"

"Forty days and forty nights." Noah turned to the others. "I hear the animals below. Go now and see to them. Be sure they are secure in their stalls, for this will be a fierce tempest."

Outside the rain was getting heavier and heavier. The crowd began to break up and turn back toward the town.

"I don't like the looks of this." Havil was wet and trembling. "I'm going home."

Sebtah grabbed his arm. "Are you afraid of a thunderstorm? It will not last long, I tell you. Noah's God is a sham—a sham!" he yelled after the now-running crowd. A blazing streak of lightning tore through the clouds and ripped into the ground in back of Sebtah. He gave a hoarse cry and ran after the retreating horde.

Black, boiling clouds blotted out the sun, casting deep shadow over the awful scene. The rain was now a streaming wall of water. Pools became lakes, and rivulets raging rivers. The waters swelled and swirled and heaved into a mighty tidal wave demolishing everything in its path.

The ark sat firm on its scaffolding amid the tumult. Shem gazed in wonder at the spectacle. "They are not laughing at us now."

"It is true they brought this destruction on themselves," said Noah, "but we must grieve for them and pray for their souls."

Japheth was also watching. "The waters are about to reach us. I must go and alert the others."

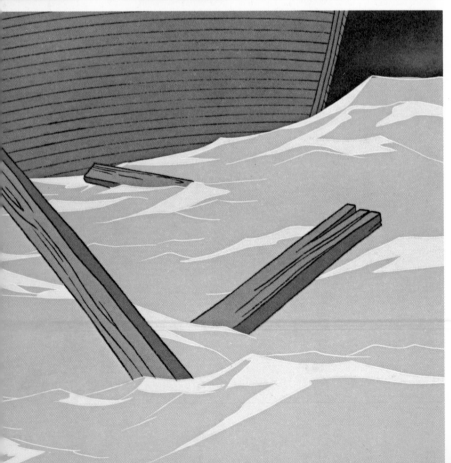

Below deck Derek already knew what was happening. "Here we go. Hang on, Moki." They grabbed an upright stanchion just in time.

The ark heeled sharply to one side as the waters tore it from the scaffolding. It went on heaving crazily, tossed by waves high as mountains.

Japheth's wife clutched at him to keep herself upright. "I cannot believe it," she shouted above the storm. "I was sure the animals would stampede, and they are not even frightened."

He held her firmly with one arm. "It is true, my dear. Look." An elephant and then a cow went sliding calmly from one side of the ark to the other.

The ark continued to heave and toss. Everyone was kept busy checking for leaks and securing the hampers and barrels and baskets, and checking the animal stalls. At last, thoroughly tired, the voyagers settled down wearily to sleep wherever they could find a dry spot.

Derek was one of the first to wake up next morning. He poked Moki. "Wake up, something is strange."

Moki bolted upright. "Man the life rafts!"

"Sh-h," Derek whispered, "why is everything so still?" They crept to a window and looked out. The ark was riding motionless on a vast sea smooth as glass, stretching to the horizon in every direction.

"Hey, everybody, the storm is over."

The shining, motionless calm continued day after day after day after day. "When will the water go down?" Shem's wife looked worried.

Noah hesitated for a long moment. "I do not know," he said.

And day after day it was the same—they got up and ate, cleaned the boat, fed the animals, cleaned the boat, ate, and went to sleep.

One morning Noah and Shem's wife went together to the storeroom. The food supply for the animals was getting very low. Noah murmured almost under his breath, "Surely God has not brought us this far without a plan to save us."

"Our supplies cannot last much longer, Father," the woman said.

Together they moved to a window and scanned the sky. Close by a raven perched, head cocked as if listening to their talk. "Here, little friend," Noah extended his hand. "Fly out over the waters for us to see if there is land." He turned to his daughter-in-law. "If he does not return, we will know he found somewhere to light."

The raven disappeared in the distance, and throughout the day anxious eyes watched for him. But the raven did not return.

Noah then released a dove. But the dove returned, having found no place to land.

Several days later Japheth took Noah below decks. "Father, our situation is serious. There is food for only a few more days. It would be better to kill some of the animals than to let them all starve. We will have to decide which ones should go first."

"Be patient a little longer, Japheth. The dove we sent out this morning has not returned, and I am sure that the good God has not saved us from the storm to let us perish in the calm."

Japheth looked sadly at the elephants and

stroked their trunks. "You will have to go first, great ones, you consume so much food."

Soft cooing made the men turn their heads. "Look, the dove has returned with a twig in its mouth, a fresh olive twig!" Noah took it gently. "God be praised. I must go and show the others."

When another week of days went by and still no land appeared, spirits began to sink.

Noah's wife tried to cheer her daughter-in-law as they were setting the food on the table. "The dove we released yesterday has not come back at all. It must have found a place to rest."

But Shem's wife was not convinced. "The bird has fallen into the sea. There is nothing but water out there."

When everyone was at the table, Noah bowed his head and prayed. "Thanks be to thee, O Lord our God, for thy blessings to us in saving us from the storm. We pray that we may be found worthy to see your clean new land. We pray that you will let us walk once more upon the earth so that we may serve you faithfully. Amen."

Everyone sat down, but jumped up again at a sharp jolt. They scurried to the windows and saw that the waters were falling rapidly. The ark had come to rest on a ledge of land with mountain peaks all around. Noah fell to his knees. "God be praised," said his wife.

The next job was to build a ramp so the animals could leave the boat. Shem and Moki went to the storeroom for lumber.

"The big storm didn't frighten you a bit, did it, Moki?" Shem teased.

"Of course not," Moki shrugged.

"And what was this for?" Shem pointed to the raft resting in the corner.

"Er, uh, I just threw it together in case one of you panicked."

Derek had joined them. "I think we can put this raft to good use now." He slapped Moki's shoulder and then turned to Shem. "We need to be on our way, and now that the water is going down we can do just that. Margo, come help us rig a sail for our little ark."

Margo was saying a fond good-bye to her friend the doe as it joined the joyous procession of animals leaving the ark.

The three friends were soon ready to take their leave. "Thanks for everything. Good-bye," Margo shouted.

"Good-bye, Mrs. Noah," said Moki.

"Good-bye, Moki. Good-bye all."

"God be with you," called the rest of the family. They had all come out of the ark to stand on dry land and wave as the little craft sailed away.

Finally Noah raised his hands. "Now let us give thanks to the Lord."

"Look!" His wife pointed to the sky. A band of soft colors glowed there, faintly at first, but growing more and more vivid, until a brilliant rainbow arched over them as they fell to their knees.

And God set his rainbow in the sky, saying, "This sign is my promise that never again will there be a flood to destroy all creatures.

"Whenever the rainbow appears in the heavens you will remember this everlasting covenant between me and all living creatures on the earth."